MATCH!

WOULD YOU RATHER?

Published 2021 by Macmillan Children's Books
an imprint of Pan Macmillan
The Smithson, 6 Briset Street, London EC1M 5NR
EU representative: Macmillan Publishers Ireland Ltd, 1st Floor,
The Liffey Trust Centre, 117–126 Sheriff Street Upper
Dublin 1, D01 YC43
Associated companies throughout the world
www.panmacmillan.com

ISBN 978-1-5290-8233-3

Text copyright © Macmillan Children's Books 2021
Illustrations copyright © Nigel Baines 2021

The right of XXX and Nigel Baines to be identified as the
author and illustrator of this work has been asserted by them
in accordance with the Copyright, Designs and Patents Act 1988.

1 3 5 7 9 8 6 4 2

A CIP catalogue record for this book is available from the British Library.

Printed and bound by CPI Group (UK) Ltd, Croydon CR0 4YY

WOULD YOU RATHER . . .

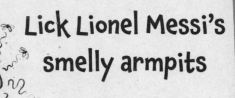

Lick Lionel Messi's smelly armpits

OR

Chew Cristiano Ronaldo's stinky socks?

WOULD YOU RATHER . . .

Pick your gaffer's nose

OR

Be left on the substitutes' bench forever?

WOULD YOU RATHER . . .

Blow snot onto your
fave footy shirt

OR

Have to swallow it?

WOULD YOU RATHER . . .

Play upfront with
Kylian Mbappé

OR

Play upfront with
Erling Haaland?

WOULD YOU RATHER . . . ?

Get hit in the face by a rocket
shot from Harry Kane

OR

Crash into the goalpost?

6

WOULD YOU RATHER . . .

Get nutmegged by
Bukayo Saka

OR

Hacked down by
Sergio Ramos?

WOULD YOU RATHER...

Sniff a rotten Bruno
Fernandes fart

OR

Miss an open goal?

WOULD YOU RATHER . . .

Face a penalty from
Ellen White

OR

Face a penalty from
Pernille Harder?

WOULD YOU RATHER . . .

Win the World Cup but
not score

OR

Win the FA Cup and hit
the winner?

WOULD YOU RATHER . . .

Score a winning penalty

OR

Save the decisive one
in a shoot-out?

WOULD YOU RATHER . . .

Have your effort hit
the corner flag

OR

Totally air-shot a sitter?

WOULD YOU RATHER . . .

Fart live on stage winning
Player Of The Year

OR

Not win Player Of
The Year at all?

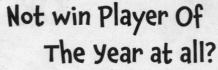

WOULD YOU RATHER . . .

Have fans chant
your name

OR

Have the most followers
on social media?

WOULD YOU RATHER . . .

Score the perfect
hat-trick

OR

Get five assists in
one game?

WOULD YOU RATHER . . .

Your team loses 5-1 but
you score a goal

OR

Your team wins 3-0
but you get sent off
without scoring?

16

WOULD YOU RATHER . . .

Score an acrobatic
bicycle-kick

OR

A 35-yard knuckleball
free kick?

WOULD YOU RATHER . . .

Have visible skid marks
on your shorts

OR

Secretly poo yourself
on the pitch?

18

WOULD YOU RATHER . . .

Lick your best mate's
football boots

OR

?

Wash your team's
kit all year?

WOULD YOU RATHER . . .

? Wear your biggest rivals' shirt for a year

OR

Never watch footy again?

?

WOULD YOU RATHER . . .

Clean boots covered
in cow poo

OR

Clean boots with tons of
chewing gum stuck
to them?

WOULD YOU RATHER . . .

Manage your
country

OR

Manage your
favourite club?

WOULD YOU RATHER . . .

Own 100 pairs of
cool boots

OR

100 jaw-dropping
shirts?

WOULD YOU RATHER . . . .

Sign a sponsorship deal
with Nike

 **OR** **?**

Sign a sponsorship deal
with Adidas?

?

WOULD YOU RATHER . . .

Earn £100,000 a game playing non-league footy

OR

Earn no money at all and play in the Premiership?

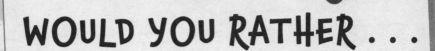

WOULD YOU RATHER . . .

Be best mates with Jadon Sancho

OR

Be best mates with
Raheem Sterling?

You're my best friend!

WOULD YOU RATHER . . .

Receive a signed shirt from
Jack Grealish

OR

A pair of signed boots from
James Maddison?

WOULD YOU RATHER . . .

Race N'Golo Kanté
over 1500 m

OR

Race Kyle Walker in a
100 m sprint?

WOULD YOU RATHER . . .

Work as a famous
TV pundit

OR

As work as your favourite
team's mascot?

WOULD YOU RATHER . . .

Play a match on the
highest mountain

OR

Play a match in the middle of
a burning desert?

WOULD YOU RATHER . . .

Be your side's ball boy
for a game

OR

Be your club's mascot
for a game?

WOULD YOU RATHER . . .

Referee a game between
Celtic and Rangers

OR

Referee a game between
Tottenham and Arsenal?

WOULD YOU RATHER . . .

Go to the toilet during a match like Eric Dier

OR

Have to hold it all game?

WOULD YOU RATHER . . .

Play 100 games at your least favourite stadium

OR

Play one game at your fave stadium?

WOULD YOU RATHER . . .

Wear two left boots

OR

Play without any boots?

WOULD YOU RATHER . . .

Score a screamer but it be
disallowed by VAR

OR

Score a tap-in and
it counts?

WOULD YOU RATHER . . .

Mow the lawn at Wembley for
the rest of your life

OR

Never have to do homework
ever again?

WOULD YOU RATHER . . .

Have your pitch invaded by 100 angry dogs

OR

Have your pitch invaded by 20 hungry crocodiles?

38

WOULD YOU RATHER . . .

Bite Sean Dyche's
nails

OR

Let him bite
yours?

WOULD YOU RATHER . . .

Lick your teammates'
sweat

OR

Never shower again?

WOULD YOU RATHER . . .

Be locked in a room with a
"hangry" Luis Suárez

OR

An angry
Romelu Lukaku?

WOULD YOU RATHER . . .

Have a team mate bite you like Luis Suárez

OR

Have to bite a teammate yourself?

WOULD YOU RATHER . . .

Score from a
corner kick

?

OR

Score from a
goal kick?

?

WOULD YOU RATHER . . .

Paint the lines of the pitch
by hand before
every game

OR

Mow the pitch lawn
every week?

44

WOULD YOU RATHER . . .

Kiss Harry Kane's socks

OR

Wear Heung-Min Son's boxers on your head for a day?

WOULD YOU RATHER . . .

Concede a goal to your
worst enemy

OR

Miss a sitter with
them in goal?

WOULD YOU RATHER . . .

Be a steward at your favourite team's ground but never watch the action

OR

Never be able to visit the stadium again?

WOULD YOU RATHER . . .

Meet a Premiership player
for five minutes

?

OR

?

Have a kick-about with a
League Two
star for a whole day?

WOULD YOU RATHER . . .

Wear Gareth Southgate's
waistcoat to a school prom

OR

Wear Jürgen Klopp's cap
to a school prom?

WOULD YOU RATHER . . .

Be sent off once for a tackle
you didn't make

OR

Get yellow carded every game for
the rest of the season?

WOULD YOU RATHER . . .

Be hit in the bum by a
Gareth Bale free kick

OR

Crash into the corner flag?

WOULD YOU RATHER . . .

Face a free kick from
James Ward-Prowse

OR

A penalty from
Bruno Fernandes?

WOULD YOU RATHER . . .

Challenge Adebayo Akinfenwa
to an arm wrestle

OR

Take on Zlatan Ibrahimović
in karate?

WOULD YOU RATHER . . .

Go viral on Tik-Tok for tripping over the ball

OR

Go viral on Tik-Tok for missing an open goal?

WOULD YOU RATHER . . .

Go back in time to play
with Marta

OR

Go back in time to play
with Kelly Smith?

WOULD YOU RATHER . . .

Smell like Phil Jones and play like Cristiano Ronaldo

OR

Smell like Cristiano Ronaldo and play like Phil Jones?

WOULD YOU RATHER . . .

Be twice the height
of Peter Crouch

OR

Half the height
of Mason Mount?

WOULD YOU RATHER . . .

Eat a burger made with mud from your local footy pitch

OR

Just eat Brussels sprouts for the rest of the year?

WOULD YOU RATHER . . .

Have an
Arturo Vidal Mohawk

OR

A Hamza Choudhury
Afro?

WOULD YOU RATHER...

Play alongside your
favourite ever player
for one game

OR

Win £1 million on
the lottery?

WOULD YOU RATHER . . .

Go a year without scoring

OR

Go a year with no eyebrows?

WOULD YOU RATHER . . .

Sell your team's best
player to your rivals
for £50 million

OR

Sell him to a team abroad
for £5 million?

WOULD YOU RATHER . . .

Be a star player in the
MLS for DC United

OR

A bench warmer in
La Liga for Real Madrid?

WOULD YOU RATHER . . .

Own Aubameyang's supercar collection and live in a shed

OR

Live in a mansion and never be allowed to leave it?

WOULD YOU RATHER . . .

Sell your team's best player
but sign two who are
just as good

OR

Point-blank refuse
to sell them?

WOULD YOU RATHER . . .

Be smacked in the face with a fish by Diego Costa

OR

Be farted on by Sergio Ramos?

SPLAT!

WOULD YOU RATHER . . .

Support a rival in your
team's league

OR

Become a
rugby fan?

WOULD YOU RATHER . . .

Slip like Steven Gerrard
in front of millions to cost your
team the league

OR

Wear underpants on your head
for the rest of your life?

WOULD YOU RATHER . . .

Share every meal you'll ever have with Steve Bruce

OR

Never be able to eat chocolate ever again?

WOULD YOU RATHER . . .

WOULD YOU RATHER . . .

Interview an angry
José Mourinho after his side
have been hammered

OR

Sleep in a haunted house
for the night?

WOULD YOU RATHER . . .

Wear shorts three
sizes too big

OR

Boots three sizes
too small?

WOULD YOU RATHER . . .

Eat Jamie Vardy's toe-nail
clippings once a week

?

OR

Smell like rubbish for the
rest of your life?

?

WOULD YOU RATHER . . .

Get fouled every time you're about to score

OR

Miss a penalty at the World Cup?

WOULD YOU RATHER . . . .

Only be able to chat to
James Milner at training
for a day

OR

Be forced to train by yourself
for a week?

WOULD YOU RATHER . . .

Play a 90-minute match in welly boots

OR

Play a 90-minute match in high heels?

WOULD YOU RATHER . . .

Sell your team's best player to your bitter rivals for half his value

OR

Sign their worst player for triple his worth?

WOULD YOU RATHER . . .

Have to send off
Diego Costa

OR

Have to send off
Carlos Tevez?

WOULD YOU RATHER . . .

Win the Champions League
with your favourite team
on Career Mode

OR

Sign Cristiano Ronaldo for
your ultimate Team?

WOULD YOU RATHER . . .

Face a free kick from
Cristiano Ronaldo

OR

Face a free kick from
Lionel Messi?

WOULD YOU RATHER . . .

Score a really
embarrassing own goal

OR

Get sent off for arguing
with the ref?

WOULD YOU RATHER . . .

Be the best player
at Stoke City

OR

Be the worst player
at Real Madrid?

WOULD YOU RATHER . . .

Be the best player at a World Cup
but your team loses in the final

OR

?

Your team win the World Cup
but you haven't played
a second all tournament?

WOULD YOU RATHER . . .?

Stand in the wall for a
David Luiz free kick

OR

Go in for a tackle with
Marcos Rojo?

WOULD YOU RATHER . . .

Celebrate by dancing like
Jesse Lingard once

OR

Have to do the dab
every single time
you score?

WOULD YOU RATHER . . .

Sing 'Sweet Caroline' in front of a sold-out Wembley stadium

OR

Have to kiss a frog?

WOULD YOU RATHER . . .

Do a smelly poo in the only toilet in the dressing room

OR

Miss a big game to go and poo at home?

WOULD YOU RATHER . . .

Wake up in the morning to find out your favourite player has retired

? OR

Wake up with one nostril?

WOULD YOU RATHER...?

Take responsibility for
losing a big game

OR

Have a teammate take
credit for a win when
you deserved it?

WOULD YOU RATHER . . .

Retire as a forgotten player
with tons of trophies

OR

Retire as a famous player
with no trophies?

MAN OF THE
MATCH

WOULD YOU RATHER . . .

your team wear a really
cool kit but play
in a run-down stadium **?**

OR

your team play in a state-of-the-art
stadium with an ugly kit?

?

WOULD YOU RATHER . . .

Be a legendary
coach

OR

Be a legendary
player?

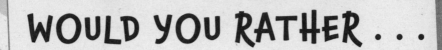

WOULD YOU RATHER . . .

Sweat an embarrassing amount

OR

Need a drink every
five minutes?

WOULD YOU RATHER . . .

Play with your best friend
for the rest of
your life

OR

Beat your rival once?

WOULD YOU RATHER . . .

Play for eight hours straight listening to an annoying mystery sound

OR

Play for eight hours straight smelling a disgusting mystery smell?

WOULD YOU RATHER . . .

Lose the ability
to pass

OR

Lose the ability
to shoot?

WOULD YOU RATHER . . .

Watch a based-on-a-true-story football film where your most hated rivals are the film's heroes

OR

Watch a based-on-a-true-story football film which glorifies your team's most heart-breaking loss ever?

WOULD YOU RATHER . . .

Have to scrub your team's
showers by hand
after a game

OR

Have to wash all of your
team's boots?

WOULD YOU RATHER . . .

Play three-a-side on a boat in the middle of the ocean

OR

Play three-a-side on a jumbo Jet up in the sky?

WOULD YOU RATHER . . .

Score an own goal

OR

Injure yourself by celebrating a goal?

WOULD YOU RATHER . . .

Eat a chunk of Mattéo Guendouzi's massive barnet

OR

Drink a glass of Gareth Bale's sweat?

WOULD YOU RATHER . . .

Be stuck in a cage with Zlatan Ibrahimović

OR

Be stuck in a cage of lions?

Help Me!

WOULD YOU RATHER . . .

?

Receive a signed shirt
from Sam Kerr

OR

Receive a pair of signed boots
from Vivianne Miedema?

?

WOULD YOU RATHER ...

Eat a chunk of
Olivier Giroud's beard

OR

Sniff his sweaty
armpits?

WOULD YOU RATHER . . .

Be caught picking your nose
during a game

OR

Be caught cleaning your ears
during a game?

WOULD YOU RATHER . . ?

Have your teammate sneeze
in your face

OR

Have your teammate blow
their nose into your
favourite shirt?

WOULD YOU RATHER . . .

?

Do an hour-long training
session in 40°C

OR

Do an hour-long training
session in -10°C?

?

WOULD YOU RATHER . . .

?

Lick the floor of a
dressing room

OR

Lick your teammate's
stinky boot?

?

WOULD YOU RATHER . . .

Fart uncontrollably during
a press conference

OR

Have to keep running
to the toilet to poo
during a game?

WOULD YOU RATHER . . .

Roll around on a
muddy pitch

OR

Roll around in
wet cement?

WOULD YOU RATHER . . .

Have Luis Suárez bite
off your ear

OR

Have Luis Suárez bite
off your nose?

WOULD YOU RATHER . . .

Have bad breath

OR

Mark someone with bad breath?

WOULD YOU RATHER . . . .

Take a shower after a game
but have to wear
dirty clothes

OR

Not take a shower but
wear clean clothes?

WOULD YOU RATHER . . .

Eat spaghetti made
from worms

OR

Eat spaghetti made from
David Luiz's hair?

WOULD YOU RATHER . . .

? Go bright purple every
time you lose the ball

OR

Sweat so much you soak
your clothes?

WOULD YOU RATHER . . .

Fart every time
you pass

OR

Burp every time
you shoot?

WOULD YOU RATHER . . .

Play football inside a Zorb ball

?

OR

Play football with a Zorb ball?

WOULD YOU RATHER . . .

Constantly feel itchy
during a game

OR

Constantly feel sticky
during a game?

WOULD YOU RATHER . . .

Play a game wearing
wet socks

OR

Spend a day with popcorn
stuck in your teeth?

WOULD YOU RATHER . . .

Hear exactly what your manager thinks of you **?**

OR

Never be able to hear them speak at all?

?

WOULD YOU RATHER . . .

? Wear an unwashed bib
for the rest of your life

OR

Wear your rival's shirt
for just one week?

WOULD YOU RATHER . . .

Run 20 laps of
Old Trafford

OR

Clean all the toilets
at the Etihad?

WOULD YOU RATHER . . .

Invent a celebration
with Dele Alli

OR

Invent a celebration with
Pierre-Emerick Aubameyang?

WOULD YOU RATHER . . .

Listen to 'You'll Never Walk Alone' on repeat for the rest of your life

OR

Listen to Man. City's 'Blue Moon' on repeat for the rest of your life?

123

WOULD YOU RATHER . . .

Appear on the front cover of
MATCH Magazine once

OR

Have a feature inside
MATCH Magazine every week
for a month?

WOULD YOU RATHER . . .

Be known for having
jaw-dropping skills

OR

Be known for
ridiculous pace?

WOULD YOU RATHER . . .

?

Have a five-star
weak foot

OR

Have five-star
skills?

WOULD YOU RATHER . . .

? Complete 2,000
kick-ups

OR

Complete 500
head-ups? ?

WOULD YOU RATHER . . .

Be told to retire from
football when you're
20 years old

OR

Be made to play football
until you're 90?

WOULD YOU RATHER . . .

High five all your teammates every time you complete a pass

OR

Get wedgies from the opposition every time you misplace a pass?

WOULD YOU RATHER . . .

Turn up to training with bog roll stuck to your shoes

OR

Turn up to training with a big bogey on your cheek?

WOULD YOU RATHER . . .

Go back in time to play
with Diego Maradona

OR

Go back in time to play
with Pele?

WOULD YOU RATHER . . .

Play alongside prime
Ronaldo R9

OR

Play alongside
Cristiano Ronaldo CR7?

WOULD YOU RATHER . . .

Have 99 rating for
strength

OR

Have 99 rating for
stamina?

WOULD YOU RATHER . . .

Be a famous football freestyler

OR

Own a famous footy fancast on YouTube?

WOULD YOU RATHER . . .

Smell Phil Foden's
shin-pads

OR

Smell Harvey
Barnes's vest?

WOULD YOU RATHER . . .

Captain your country to a
World Cup final but lose

OR

Be an unused substitute in a
World Cup final and win?

WOULD YOU RATHER . . .

Be made to do 100 push-ups at training

OR

Be made to do 100 sit-ups?

WOULD YOU RATHER . . .

Spend a day locked in a lift with Gareth Southgate

OR

?

Spend a week locked in a changing room with José Mourinho?

WOULD YOU RATHER . . . .

Be a football shirt designer

OR

Be a football boot designer?

WOULD YOU RATHER . . .

? Play with a totally
flat football

OR

Play with a football filled
with stones? **?**

WOULD YOU RATHER . . .

Abseil down Tottenham's stadium

OR

Bungee jump off the Emirates?

WOULD YOU RATHER . . .

Feature on MATCH's social media channels

OR

Feature on MATCH's front cover?

WOULD YOU RATHER . . .

Drink two litres of energy drinks
before a game

OR

Eat ten packs of
energy snacks?

WOULD YOU RATHER . . .

Have Lionel Messi's dribbling ability

OR

Have Cristiano Ronaldo's finishing?

WOULD YOU RATHER . . .

Have Virgil van Dijk's
tackling tekkers

OR

Have Toni Kroos's
passing range?

WOULD YOU RATHER . . .

Miss your team's final through injury

OR

Be stung
by a
massive
bee?

WOULD YOU RATHER . . .

Have Romelu Lukaku's strength

OR

?

Have Tomáš Souček's aerial ability?

?

WOULD YOU RATHER . . .

Have Jan Oblak's
reflexes

OR

Have Trent Alexander-Arnold's
crossing ability?

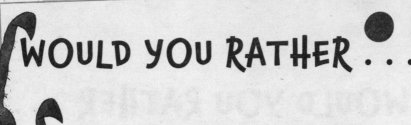

WOULD YOU RATHER . . .

Wear three pairs of football socks for a game

OR

Wear three pairs of shorts?

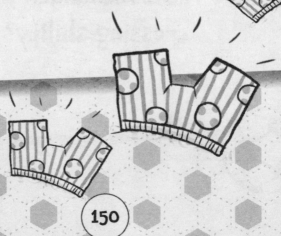

WOULD YOU RATHER . . .

Be nicknamed
'The Jewell'

OR

Be nicknamed
'The Boss'?

WOULD YOU RATHER . . .

Be best mates with
Ansu Fati

OR

?

Be best mates with
Vinícius Junior?

?

152

WOULD YOU RATHER . . .

Get a tattoo of your rival club's crest on your toe

?

OR

Get a tattoo of your favourite club's crest on your forehead?

?

153

WOULD YOU RATHER . . .

Be Cristiano Ronaldo's agent

OR

Be Cristiano Ronaldo's best mate?

WOULD YOU RATHER . . .

Be forced to wear goalkeeper
gloves for the rest
of your life

OR

Be forced to wear shin-pads for
the rest of your life?

WOULD YOU RATHER . . .

Be named Player Of The Season
by your teammates

OR

Be named Player Of The Season
by your manager?

156

WOULD YOU RATHER . . .

Be allergic to grass

OR

Be allergic to clothes?

WOULD YOU RATHER . . .

Have your dad as
your agent

OR

Your best mate as
your agent?

WOULD YOU RATHER . . .

Play for your favourite club
and earn nothing

OR

Move to China and earn
£500,000 a week?

WOULD YOU RATHER . . . ?

Score an overhead
kick in the park

OR

Assist a goal in a
competitive match?

WOULD YOU RATHER . . .

Eat an orange at
half-time

?

OR

Eat a meat pie at
half-time?

?

WOULD YOU RATHER . . .

ONE SHEET PER PERSON

Every football shirt you ever wear be itchy

OR

Only be able to use one piece of toilet paper every time you go to the loo?

WOULD YOU RATHER . . .

Shout everything you think in the dressing room

OR

Sing everything you think in the dressing room?

WOULD YOU RATHER . . .

Be unable to move your body every time you play in the rain

OR

Not be able to stop moving when the sun is out?

WOULD YOU RATHER . . .

Have a water-balloon war in the dressing room at full time

OR ?

Have a food fight in the dressing room at full time?

WOULD YOU RATHER . . .

Have Lauren Hemp's
dribbling ability

OR

Have Chloe Kelly's
finishing ability?

WOULD YOU RATHER . . .

Become twice as strong when both of your fingers are stuck in your ears

OR

Dribble twice as fast when your fingers are stuck in your ears?

WOULD YOU RATHER . . .

WOULD YOU RATHER . . .

Be a world-class
player

OR

Be a world-class
manager?

168

WOULD YOU RATHER . . .

Be your favourite club's admin on social media

OR

Be your favourite club's chief executive?

WOULD YOU RATHER . . .

Fart loudly every time you have a
serious conversation with
your manager

OR

Burp every
time you
make a pass?

WOULD YOU RATHER . . .

Live in your favourite
club's stadium

OR

Live in your favourite club's
training ground?

WOULD YOU RATHER . . .

?

Play a game without
a referee

OR

Have to wear exactly the same kit
as your opponent?

WOULD YOU RATHER . . .

Be unable to pass

OR

Be unable to shoot?

WOULD YOU RATHER . . .

Be a world-class player with
a bright orange topknot

OR

Be an average player with
a boring haircut?

WOULD YOU RATHER . . .

Never get stuck in traffic on the way to a game

OR

Never get another cold?

WOULD YOU RATHER . . .

Be forced to eat only spicy food before a game

OR

Be forced to eat only incredibly boring food?

WOULD YOU RATHER . . . ?

Be fantastic at taking
free kicks

OR

Amazing at taking
penalties?

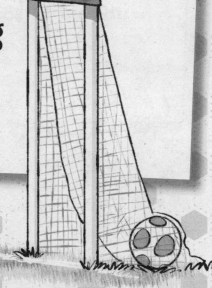

WOULD YOU RATHER . . .

Eat a sandwich made from four ingredients in your fridge chosen at random

OR

Eat a sandwich made by a group of your teammates from four ingredients in your fridge?

WOULD YOU RATHER . . .

Never be able to wear your football shirt

OR

Never be able to wear shorts?

WOULD YOU RATHER . . .

Never be able to
make a pass

OR

Never be able to make
a tackle?

WOULD YOU RATHER ...

Get to go to the Champions League final every year for free

OR

Be able to watch a League Two game every week?

WOULD YOU RATHER . . .

Give up playing football
for a month

OR

Give up watching football
for a month?

WOULD YOU RATHER . . .

Never be able to watch your favourite team play again

OR

Only be able to watch your team play and nobody else?

WOULD YOU RATHER . . .

Never get fouled again

OR

Never get something stuck in your teeth again?

WOULD YOU RATHER . . .

Never miss an open goal in front of your mates again

 OR

Never feel the need to fart in public again?

WOULD YOU RATHER . . .

your team sold their
star player

OR

your team sold every single
player other than their
star player?

WOULD YOU RATHER . . .

Play a game against your mates in continuous snow

OR

Play a game against your mates in continuous rain?

WOULD YOU RATHER . . .

Vomit uncontrollably for one minute every time you score a goal

OR

Get a headache that lasts for the rest of the day every time you assist a goal?

WOULD YOU RATHER . . .

Never have to clean your boots again

OR

Never have to track back and defend again?

WOULD YOU RATHER . . .

WOULD YOU RATHER . . .

Be able to go to any football
game in the world for free
for the rest of your life

?

OR

Eat for free at any drive-through
restaurant for the rest of your life?

?

WOULD YOU RATHER . . .

Never sweat again

OR

Never feel cold again?

WOULD YOU RATHER . . .

Have constantly dry eyes
during a game

OR

?

Have a constant runny nose?

?

WOULD YOU RATHER . . .

Lose all your football
shirts

OR

Lose all your
football boots?

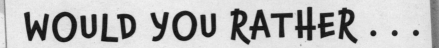

WOULD YOU RATHER . . .

Be able to control your
manager's decisions

OR

Be able to control the
referee's decisions?

WOULD YOU RATHER . . .

Sign for your favourite club
for nothing

OR

Find a suitcase with
£5 million inside?

WOULD YOU RATHER . . .

Always be alone in the dressing room after a game

OR

Always be surrounded by annoying people after a game?

WOULD YOU RATHER . . .

Be responsible for your side losing a game in stoppage time

OR

Be responsible for accidentally injuring your side's best player?

WOULD YOU RATHER . . .

Never be able to use
social media again

OR

Never be able to watch a
football game again?

198

WOULD YOU RATHER . . .

Have someone throw up on your favourite football shirt

OR

Have to throw up on someone else's football shirt?

WOULD YOU RATHER . . .

Be able to jump up to
five metres

OR

Sprint at the speed
of light?

WOULD YOU RATHER . . .

Hear a referee's whistle
every hour

OR

Hear a vuvuzela every
two hours?

WOULD YOU RATHER . . . ?

Play 100 games for your country's youth teams but never win a senior cap

OR

Play 0 games for the youth teams and just one for the senior side?

WOULD YOU RATHER . . .

Play a game with your shirt
inside out

OR

Play a game with your shirt
back to front?

WOULD YOU RATHER . . .

Play for
Argentina

OR

Play for
Brazil?

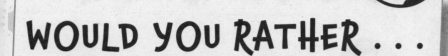

WOULD YOU RATHER . . .

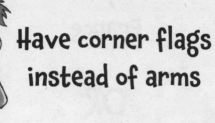

Have corner flags instead of arms

OR

Have two goalposts instead of legs?

WOULD YOU RATHER . . .

Play for
France

OR

Play for
Germany?

WOULD YOU RATHER . . .

Represent the Netherlands

OR

Represent Belgium?

WOULD YOU RATHER . . .

Represent
Spain

OR

Represent
Portugal?

?

?

WOULD YOU RATHER . . .

Play for
Inter Milan

OR

Play for
AC Milan?

WOULD YOU RATHER . . .

?

Play for
Celtic

OR

Play for
Rangers?

?

WOULD YOU RATHER . . .

Play for
Borussia Dortmund

OR

Play for
Bayern Munich?

WOULD YOU RATHER . . .

Crowd surf at the San Siro

OR

Crowd surf at Marseille's Vélodrome?

WOULD YOU RATHER . . .

Play for Olympiacos

OR

Play for Fenerbahçe?

WOULD YOU RATHER . . .

Score nine shots
out of ten

OR

Win nine games
out of ten?

WOULD YOU RATHER . . .

Complete the most dribbles
in your league

OR

Be the most accurate shooter
in your league?

WOULD YOU RATHER . . .

Give Steve Bruce a
piggyback

OR

Give Rafa Benítez a
foot boost?

WOULD YOU RATHER . . .

Spend a week learning tactics
off Pep Guardiola

OR

Spend a week learning tactics
off Jürgen Klopp?

WOULD YOU RATHER . . .

Be taught how to shoot
by Erling Haaland

OR

Be taught how to defend
by Virgil van Dijk?

WOULD YOU RATHER . . .

Have hands that keep growing
every time you make a pass

?

OR

Have feet that keep growing
every time you make a pass?

WOULD YOU RATHER . . .

Have over 10 million followers on social media

OR

Have 0 followers but get to be a mascot for your favourite team for a day?

WOULD YOU RATHER . . .

Jump in a hot tub with a
farting Sadio Mané

OR

Spend an hour in a sauna with
a sweating Mohamed Salah?

WOULD YOU RATHER . . .

Be able to speak ten languages fluently

OR

Get to take one penalty against Ederson?

WOULD YOU RATHER . . .

Lose all of your football ability and never be able to get it back

OR

Be woken up every day for the rest of your life by Mason Mount screaming?

WOULD YOU RATHER . . .

Only eat gone-off food for
the rest of your life

OR

Be wedgied every day
by Paul Pogba?

WOULD YOU RATHER . . .

Play the rest of your life with an
in-grown toe-nail

OR

Play the rest of your life with a
blister on your heel?

WOULD YOU RATHER . . .

Nibble Alexandre Lacazette's beard

OR

Eat a handful of his chest hair?

WOULD YOU RATHER . . .

Never be able to play football video games

?

OR

?

Never be able to watch TV again?

WOULD YOU RATHER . . .

Get an electric shock every time you miss a chance

OR

Get an electric shock every time you give the ball away?

WOULD YOU RATHER . . .

Never be able to play
football again

OR ?

Never be able to leave your
house again?

WOULD YOU RATHER . . .

Be able to pull off the perfect Sombrero skill

OR ?

?

Be able to pull off the perfect Elastico?

WOULD YOU RATHER . . .

Win the European
Championship

OR

Finish runners-up in
the World Cup?

WOULD YOU RATHER . . . .

?

Have a season ticket in
the Yellow Wall
at Borussia Dortmund

OR

Have a season ticket in
the Kop at Anfield?

?

WOULD YOU RATHER . . .

Have a season ticket in
the Stretford End at
Manchester United

OR

Have a season ticket in the
Shed End at Chelsea?

WOULD YOU RATHER . . .

Watch a documentary on your favourite club

OR

Help film a documentary on your club's biggest rivals?

WOULD YOU RATHER . . .

Have everyone laugh at your dressing room jokes but not find anyone else's jokes funny

OR

Have nobody laugh at your dressing room jokes but you still find other people's jokes funny?

WOULD YOU RATHER . . .

Wake up in the middle of a boggy pitch

OR

Wake up in a smelly dressing room?

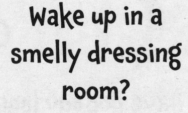

WOULD YOU RATHER . . .

Run around the pitch for the whole game without realizing there is a giant brown stain on the back of your shorts

OR

Realize the deadline for Fantasy Football was yesterday, and you forgot to check your team?

WOULD YOU RATHER . . . .

Be so afraid of heights that you can't challenge for headers

OR

Be so afraid of the sun that you can only play on rainy days?

WOULD YOU RATHER . . .

Go down as one of the most famous players in history

OR

Be forgotten as soon as you retire?

WOULD YOU RATHER . . .

Be popular with your manager

OR

Be popular with your teammates?

240

WOULD YOU RATHER . . .

Your boots always be two sizes too big **?**

OR

Your boots always be two sizes too small?

?

WOULD YOU RATHER . . .

Find £10 on the ground

OR

Find all your missing
football socks
on the ground?

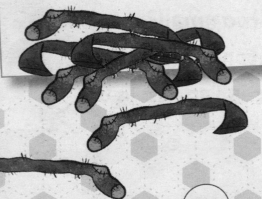

WOULD YOU RATHER . . .

Push a lawn-mower around the pitch with a handle that is far too high

OR

Push a lawn-mower around the pitch with a handle that is far too low?

WOULD YOU RATHER . . .

Always feel like someone is tackling you, but nobody is

OR

Always feel like someone is chasing you, even though nobody is?

DON'T MISS THESE OTHER

EPIC MATCH! BOOKS